MARGARET MORGAN
and
MARY MORGAN PEDLOW

Memorial

RIVERSIDE PUBLIC LIBRARY

LIFE DURING THE
GREAT CIVILIZATIONS

The Song Dynasty

Scott Ingram

BLACKBIRCH®
PRESS

THOMSON

GALE

San Diego • Detroit • New York • San Francisco • Cleveland • New Haven, Conn. • Waterville, Maine • London • Munich

LIBRARY OF CONGRESS CATALOGING-IN-PUBLICATION DATA

Ingram, Scott.
  The Song dynasty / By Scott Ingram.
    p. cm. — (Life during the great civilizations)
Includes bibliographical references and index.
  ISBN 1-4103-0056-0 (alk. paper)
  1. China—Civilization—960-1644—Juvenile literature. 2. China—History—Song dynasty, 960-1279—Juvenile literature. I. Title. II. Series.

  DS750.72.I54 2004
  951'.024—dc21   2003014718

Printed in United States
10 9 8 7 6 5 4 3 2 1

Contents

INTRODUCTION

The Dawn of the Modern World

Other than Egypt and India, no modern nation has a longer history than China, the world's most populous nation and the second-largest country in the world. Chinese civilization began almost seven thousand years ago in China Proper, a region in eastern China between the country's two main rivers, the Yellow and the Yangtze. With fertile soil, adequate rainfall, and moderate temperatures, China Proper was an ideal location for the development of agriculture and transportation, the building blocks of Chinese society.

Over the course of its history, China has been controlled by ruling families that passed down their power through generations. Although there were many kingdoms in China over the centuries, only a few were powerful enough to unite other kingdoms under one ruler—an emperor. In Chinese history, the rule of an emperor and his descendants is known as a dynasty.

The fertile region known as China Proper, between the Yellow and Yangtze Rivers, was the birthplace of Chinese civilization.

The first dynasty to rule virtually all of China was the Qin in 221 B.C. "Qin" was originally written in English as "Ch'in," which is believed to be the origin of the word China. For more than nine hundred years, China was ruled by emperors who considered their subjects little more than slaves. By the middle of the ninth century, natural disasters, warfare, and peasant rebellions had caused the ruling dynasty to collapse. In 960, however, the Song (SOOng) dynasty arose from the turmoil and unified most of China.

The reign of the Song dynasty was divided into two phases, the Northern Song, who ruled from 960 to 1127, and the Southern Song, who ruled from 1127 to 1279. When the Song arose, Chinese civilization was almost six thousand years old. Tradition was important to the Chinese, and the rulers of the new dynasty had a deep respect for their country's past.

What separated the new rulers from previous emperors, however, was their concern for all citizens, not just a small circle of family and wealthy nobility. While there was suffering among the poorest Chinese, the Song era offered economic and educational opportunities that were unavailable anywhere else in the world at that time. The dynasty's strength arose from an economy based on peaceful trade rather than expansion through military conquest, the previous measure of power. For that reason, the Song dynasty is considered one of the first great modern civilizations.

Unlike their predecessors, rulers of the Song dynasty offered their citizens greater educational opportunities than those anywhere else in the world at that time.

CHAPTER ONE

A New Kind of Government

Despite its modern reputation as a peaceful civilization, the Song dynasty emerged in a time of warfare and rebellion. The dynasty that directly preceded the Song, the Tang, fell in 907, and its collapse led to a period of civil war between regions as well as foreign invasion.

One dynasty that emerged briefly during this period was the later Zhou. The Zhou controlled a relatively small region of northern China, and through the efforts of its well-trained army, it was able to drive foreign invaders back beyond China's borders. The commanding general of the Zhou forces was named Zhao Kuangyin. Zhao, born in 927, was descended from a long line of military leaders. His father and grandfather had both been commanding generals in the Tang dynasty.

With the threat of foreign conquest removed, many troops who served under Zhao saw him as the man to lead the dynasty to greater power. In 960, Zhao's troops requested that he take the throne for himself. Zhao, who was just thirty-two years old, was reluctant to take on such a large responsibility, but he agreed to do so with the condition that his troops agree not to destroy personal property, harm citizens, or injure the ruling family in the takeover. From then on, he was known as the emperor Taizu, and the dynasty he ruled was called the Song.

During the early years of the Song, Taizu sent his armed forces from one kingdom to another to unite them under the dynasty's rule. These missions were far different from

Zhao Kuangyin, a descendant of a long line of military leaders, became the first emperor of the Song dynasty in A.D. 960. As emperor, he was known as Taizu.

previous violent conquests that had torn China apart. Song troops refused to harm local populations and offered pardons to any local military governors who gave up their positions.

The governors were replaced by civilian officials who had qualified for their positions through a rigorous set of tests called imperial examinations. The tests were based on the writings of the famous Chinese philosopher Confucius, whose teachings had been written down in books known as the *Five Classics* and the *Four Books.*

The Examination System

When they based the tests on Confucian teachings, the early Song rulers did not break new ground. Examinations for government service based on Confucian teaching had been used as far back as the Qin dynasty in 221 B.C., but until the Song, only nobility had access to the written works. Thus, until the Song, the examination system reinforced the hold of the wealthy few over the majority of Chinese people.

Taizu, who had insisted on making his own way in his military career, felt that opening the exam system to all citizens would allow them opportunities regardless of wealth or family ties. During his reign, wood-block printing was invented in China, and printing presses using movable blocks of type could produce books at a relatively rapid pace, which made them more widely available. At first, the books were sold in bookstores operated by the government, but as the economy grew, retired government officials and scholars opened private businesses that bought and sold books.

As in the past, the tests were extremely difficult and required years of study. It was not unusual for men to take the exams from youth until old age before they passed them. Some men became so upset at repeated failures, they committed suicide rather than face their family

and friends. Yet this did not discourage men from taking the yearly exams, which were given at the local, provincial, and national levels with test takers shut in tiny rooms no larger than a jail cell.

Local exams lasted twenty-four hours and tested candidates on their overall knowledge of the classics, the ability to write poetry, and their skill in an artistic form of penmanship called calligraphy. Passing this test was considered admirable, but it meant only that a candidate could now take the examination at the next level.

At the provincial level, a candidate's success depended on the flawless memorization of the Confucian classics before a test that lasted two days. A candidate who passed this level was called a juren, which means "recommended candidate," and was eligible to take the national-level exams. Men preparing for the national exam virtually disappeared from day-to-day family life in order to study.

次 四 闕 求 蒲 文 嚮 技 於 於 降 築 之 儒 仲 石 汉 韓 令
安 夷 上 之 輪 而 興 於 賈 奴 霽 斯 飯 得 雅 舒 建 黥 安 則 趙
府 未 方 如 迎 歡 人 弓 豎 僕 斯 牛 人 於 則 兒 石 卜 國 鄭 禹
庫 賓 欲 弗 於 息 並 枕 衛 日 亦 之 於 人 公 寬 慧 式 慮

For the seventy-two-hour national examination, candidates demonstrated their knowledge of the classics as well as their knowledge of current topics that included law, state ceremonies, and military strategy. The emperor himself presided over the examination, and a candidate who passed the national level entered the highest level of society except for nobility or royalty—the *jinshi*, or honorable scholar.

The New Laws

The development of the new scholar class, drawn from many different levels of society, brought enormous changes to the government. Educated men now occupied positions of respect. Instead of fierce warriors or corrupt nobles who sought power only for personal gain, government officials such as Cheng Yi wrote: "Compared with sacrificing one's moral standing, starving to death is as nothing."[1]

Because Song rulers and officials followed the principles of Confucius, their major focus became the well-being of the people. In the mid–eleventh century, for example, an official named Wang An-shih convinced his emperor, Shen Zong, to adopt a program he called the *hsin fa* (*shin fah*), or new laws.

Under the tax system of the *hsin fa*, the agricultural produce of each province was used first to pay the imperial taxes and then to pay for the public works in that province such as canals, bridges and road repair. Surplus crops were bought by the government and stored in case of poor future harvests.

Under the *hsin fa*, troop levels were reduced and unneeded soldiers were sent home, in most cases to become farmers. In their place, a citizen militia was formed and the responsibility for defense of the dynasty was largely given to the civilians.

During his years in office, Wang also persuaded the emperor that the government should take charge of the care of elderly people, provide free burial to the poor, and assume responsibility for orphanages. To obtain the money for these services, all taverns were run by the government, and taxes were raised on the wealthiest citizens.

Wang believed that his actions reflected the teachings of Confucius, but his policies were not popular with the upper class. Conservative scholars and wealthy nobles believed the government had assumed too much responsibility for the common people. True Confucianism, they claimed, required each person to assume personal responsibility for his or her actions. After Wang's death, the tension between the citizens who benefited from his programs and the conservative Confucians weakened public support of the dynasty, which in turn weakened the dynasty militarily.

The decline occurred gradually until the mid-1200s. After almost three centuries of relative peace, scholar-officials of the Song decided a powerful military was unnecessary. They believed that their political,

This painting depicts scholars as they collate Confucian texts. Emperor Taizu and other Song rulers followed Confucian principles that urged government's care for its people.

The Love of Books

Not surprisingly, the love of books and reading became a prominent value as the Song dynasty evolved. This poem, written by Emperor Renzong, who ruled from 1023 to 1063, is an example of the high regard in which books were held.

To enrich your family, there is no need to buy good land:

Books hold a thousand measures of grain.

For an easy life, there is no need to build a mansion:

In books are found houses of gold.

When you go out, do not be upset if no one follows you:

In books there will be a crowd of horses and carriages.

If you wish to marry, don't be upset if you [have no one]:

In books there are girls with faces like jade.

A young man who wishes to be somebody

—will devote his time to the Classics.

He will face the window and read.

The Mongol king Ghengis Khan conquered much of China Proper during the mid–thirteenth century.

economic, and cultural accomplishments would convince enemies to leave them in peace. Should war break out, they were confident that the citizen militia could defend the dynasty's borders.

The flaw in those beliefs had been demonstrated in 1126, however, when the dynasty fled from its capital in Kaifeng to Hangzhou after northern China was conquered by Mongols. Despite the Song forces' use of gunpowder in cannons, the inexperienced fighters of the militia were no match for the well-trained cavalry of the invaders. Despite the defeat, rulers refused to believe that a government based on Confucian principles could fall.

Over the next 150 years, however, the Southern Song's borders were constantly threatened by Mongols, who slaughtered entire populations of distant provinces. This caused terror across China, and the Song rulers quickly lost all support. By the mid–thirteenth century, the Mongol king Genghis Khan had conquered much of China Proper as well as western China and western Asia. His son, Kublai Khan, eventually conquered Hangzhou and established a Mongol dynasty, the Yuan, to replace the Song in 1279.

不對田賦
季孫欲以田賦訪諸仲尼仲尼
不對而私語冉有曰君子之度丁
禮施取其厚事舉其中斂從其
薄若貪冒無厭則雖以田賦將
又不足又何訪焉

CHAPTER TWO

Confucianism in Everyday Life

Although the Song dynasty was constantly under threat from distant regions, it created economic growth as well as great artistic, scientific, and intellectual achievements previously unknown in China. For most Chinese, the firm foundation of the Song success was its devotion to Confucian thought and the certainty that it represented the core values of all Chinese, rich or poor.

Foundation of Chinese Culture

Kongfuzi, whose name was spelled "Confucius" in English, was born in 551 B.C. in northeastern China. During his childhood, the early Zhou dynasty was crumbling, and many of its social traditions and ethical values were widely questioned. Eventually, the Zhou fell and China sank into almost endless warfare during Confucius's life.

Throughout this turbulent period, Confucius traveled across China and spoke publicly about his philosophy, while followers wrote down his words. Much of his teaching centered on the proper relation between the government and its citizens. Confucius compared the citizen-ruler relationship to that of a family. In the family view he presented, the children live morally upright lives and unquestioningly obey their parents, who make decisions based on their superior understanding of what is best for the family in order for everyone to succeed.

Confucius, depicted between two disciples in this painting, traveled throughout China to teach his philosophies. He believed that the citizen-ruler relationship was like a family relaitonship.

Although he had many devoted followers in his lifetime, Confucius's teachings had little impact until more than two centuries after his death in 479 B.C. During the reign of the Han dynasty (206 B.C.–A.D. 1220), his philosophy as written down in the classics was used to form the foundation of the early dynasty's political and social system. Over many centuries, in various interpretations, the ideas of Confucius became part of Chinese culture.

Plan for Living

For Song dynasty subjects who were poor, illiterate farmers in rural areas, Confucianism did not come from books. Instead, traditions passed down over the centuries provided guides for daily life. In general, those who followed the ideals believed that self-improvement was the key to happiness.

That happiness, however, was beneficial only if it helped create better lives for others. There was no religious or inner-focused meditation necessary to follow the teachings. In fact, individuality went against Confucian philosophy. Becoming a better person meant serving one's family, village, province, or government.

A New Arrangement

This general belief tied in well with the new style of government. As the number of educated officials rose at every level, entire regions developed along the lines of Confucian thought. People agreed to this development not because they feared the emperor but because they trusted a government guided by Confucian thought.

Much of that trust stemmed from the fact that the government had improved the lives of its citizens. The first step to improve life was to provide enough food for all. The basic food was rice, a grain that required a great deal of labor to raise but that produced more nutrition per acre than any other food.

Foot Binding

There are many legends that explain the origin of foot binding. One tells of a ruler who delighted in watching women dance on their toes and then forced his daughters to bind their feet to resemble the tiny feet of the dancers on their toes.

The process of binding the feet began when girls were between the ages of four and seven. A long bandage was wrapped tightly around the feet, forcing the four small toes on each foot under the sole. This bowed the arch of the foot and forced the big toe and the heel closer together. The bandage was tightened each day while the girl's feet were put into

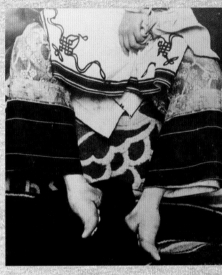

Foot binding so disfigured a woman's feet that she was barely able to walk.

smaller and smaller shoes. The entire process usually took about two years, at the end of which the feet were essentially dead and useless. Women with bound feet were barely able to walk and were thus confined to the home.

Built during the Song dynasty, this post office building still stands today. The distribution of printed relationship provided a link between the government and the people.

Under the Song rule, educated officials collected data on the methods used by the most successful farmers in their districts. The information was printed in manuals and distributed to every district. Because Song officials were required to be literate, they were able to convey the information and help all farmers succeed.

In addition to the distribution of printed material, the development of a thriving iron industry in Song cities led to the mass production of iron farming implements such as plows, hoes, and shovels to replace wooden tools. Song officials made inexpensive loans to farmers to enable them to buy these tools, and this helped create a bond between the country and city population as they became interdependent.

The key contribution of the Song government, however, was its policy of open borders. This permitted a new type of rice that grew twice as fast as other rice to be imported from southeast Asia into southern China. Farmers were able to grow two crops each year, one of rice and one of a cash crop that they could sell in the cities. This eventually led to a city-based economic system that benefited all levels of society.

Community Organization

With the support of people in rural areas, Song rulers were able to organize communities according to Confucian principles. Using the model of obedience, the officials selected a respected elder in each village or community to take responsibility for making certain that strict codes of behavior were followed.

At monthly village meetings, the actions of each family were evaluated by the elder. Villagers were expected to congratulate neighbors on a birth or other happy occasion and express sympathy for losses. People were expected to help one another during harvests as well as during floods and other misfortunes. Families whose actions were criticized could suffer the most serious punishment possible under the Confucian system: banishment from the community.

Rice was the basic food of China. During the Song dynasty, rice production doubled due to improved farming techniques and the open-borders policy.

Homes in the Song Era

Whether a family was rich or poor, homes built during the Song dynasty shared many similarities. For example, all houses were built facing south to shield people from cold northern winds. The foundations of houses were usually made of dirt pounded into walls or shaped into bricks. Roofs were usually clay tiles, although the poorest people used straw and bamboo for roofs. Most houses included an enclosed courtyard whose size revealed the wealth of a family.

One of the most important spaces in all Chinese homes, usually in the main room of the house, was a shrine that honored the family's ancestors. According to Confucian belief, people are required to honor not only living elders but also the dead. As a result, all Chinese families, rich or poor, devoted a space to ancestor worship, where offerings of food and incense were placed.

This twelfth-century painting depicts the Confucian belief that children should show respect and obedience to all adults.

The other important part of the Chinese home was found in the bedroom, where a raised sleeping platform called a *kang* was located. In cold weather, the *kang* was heated by air vents connected to nearby coal-burning stoves. This was the only heated area in the home, and was thus a place where family activities took place in cold weather.

Family Life in Song Times

Family life was also built on Confucian belief. All family members, especially the children, were expected to show unquestioning obedience to adults. The oldest male had absolute power in his household, and it was considered within his rights for him to kill his wife or children if they disobeyed or dishonored the family name.

The father also arranged the marriage of his children, which was often decided when the children were infants. Young people had no

Religion in the Song Dynasty

A number of religions were prominent during the Song era. The main Chinese religion was Taoism, which originated in the teachings of the philosopher Lao-tzu, who lived at roughly the same time as Confucius.

The word *Tao* means "the path" or "the way," and, like Confucians, Taoists seek to understand their relationship to the world around them. Where Confucians see the relationships within families and between society and the state as the way to happiness, Taoists believe in the order and harmony of nature.

The other main religion of the Song era was Buddhism, which originated in India and was brought to China in about A.D. 1220. Like Taoism, Buddhism teaches that an inner focus is the path to happiness. Zen beliefs emphasize that all people have the ability to achieve happiness but most people do not realize it.

Although the basic beliefs of both Taoism and Buddhism are opposed to the Confucian teachings of duty and respect in the family and in society, Song scholars were open-minded enough to tolerate both to a certain degree.

say in the arrangement, and most matches were made to benefit the wealth or social status of families.

Although the power of husband and father had a long tradition in China, the Song era brought some changes to family life, in particular the attitude toward women. According to traditional Confucian principles, a woman is required to obey her husband or older males in the extended family.

Women of the Song era differed somewhat from that tradition, largely due to the greater opportunities available to men. Those men who wished to advance had to study constantly if they hoped to pass the imperial examinations. The long hours of study by men required women to take over the work previously done by husbands and sons. In rural areas, women had farming responsibilities along with traditional household tasks. In cities, it was not uncommon for women to be in charge of shops, stalls, or other family businesses.

Despite the fact that Confucian beliefs require women to obey men, in the Song society they gained new rights. Widows were allowed to remarry and had the right to inherit property. Wives had the right to control family budgets and make decisions regarding their children's education.

Nevertheless, while women played an important role in Song society, they were far from equal. For example, despite their participation in the working life of the society, women were not allowed to have an education or to be paid for work they did.

CHAPTER THREE

The Largest City in the World

Most great civilizations are known for their cities, and, by 1100 A.D., Kaifeng, the capital of the Song dynasty, was the most spectacular city in the world. Located in the modern province of Henan, southwest of Beijing, Kaifeng's population was more than five hundred thousand—the largest city in the world at that time.

Besides population, Kaifeng differed from other cities in significant ways. Most cities at that time were protected by walls, gates, and water barriers such as moats. Kaifeng, too, was circled by walls. In fact, the city had three walls. One separated the imperial city, which housed the emperor, from the inner city. Another was built between the inner and outer city, which was in turn surrounded by a third outer wall. In Kaifeng, however, the walls had no defensive purpose. Commercial activity took place around the clock, so the gates to the inner city were never closed.

Four water gates along the inner and outer city walls allowed passage on waterways to and from the twelve-hundred-mile-long Grand Canal, the country's main supply route, which was a mile outside of the city. Along the banks of the waterways stood rows of warehouses filled with rice and goods from distant areas of China. Camel caravans of traders and merchants also came to Kaifeng with perfume, musical instruments, jewelry, and other rare items.

This ink drawing depicts an entry gate to Kaifeng, the Song dynasty's capital city. With more than half a million residents, Kaifeng was the largest city in the world in A.D. 1001.

Painting Tells the Story

Merchants brought their goods to and from Kaifeng along the Grand Canal (pictured), the twelve-hundred-mile-long waterway that was China's main supply route.

The color and excitement of life in Kaifeng made it a favorite place for painters to gather. Although books and writers were widely admired during the Song dynasty, painting was the most respected of all creative arts, and many people consider the Song era the greatest period of Chinese painting.

Many painters created detailed scenes to capture the busy pace of life in the largest city in the world. Some paintings show workmen in ragged clothes who unloaded sacks of rice from transport boats on the waterways. Others show that inside the city walls, merchants raised signs above their shops that advertised their products or services. Shops that sold medicinal herbs had signs such as "Care for the Five Wounds and Seven Injuries and Deficiencies of Speech." Perfume sellers offered "Genuine Prescriptions of the Collected Fragrances Remedy."

While many merchants operated from storefronts surrounding the central square, there were also vendors in temporary stalls. One of the most crowded stalls was that of the fortune-teller, who played an important role in the Song world. People from every level of society—

nobles, scholars, and workers—relied on these men to determine the best time for important family events. Using cards, tea leaves, or celestial charts, fortune-tellers told their clients the best day to open a business, bury the dead, or take a trip.

City scenes also portray the different classes of people who mingled in the marketplace. The lowest members of society, peasants who performed manual labor, wore coarse hemp clothing. Often they carried loads in baskets that hung from long poles balanced on their shoulders. They used pole baskets because they could not afford the expense of caring for an animal to help them.

At a higher economic level, farmers and merchants hauled their goods in two-wheeled carts pulled by donkeys. Larger wagons were pulled by oxen, the sign of a more successful person. Horses were generally ridden by only scholars and *jinshi* officials, who could

A painting depicts the activity of Kaifeng's bustling marketplace. Song-era Kaifeng attracted a large number of artists in what many consider the greatest period of Chinese painting.

afford to keep such animals. Camels were the beasts of burden used by foreign traders.

At the highest level of society, wealthy nobles and royalty were carried on chairs or litters. In general, women rode in sedan chairs covered with curtains to keep out the dust as well as to avoid curious stares from the lower-class throngs. In truth, upper-class women only went out in public on certain holidays or for special events. Most women shown in city scenes are shop clerks or customers.

Song royalty rode through the city in litters (pictured) or on chairs held aloft by servants.

The homes that appear in paintings of Kaifeng and other cities were constructed in much the same way as those in rural areas, and their size depended on family wealth. In cities, however, the homes of scholars or nobles often had elaborate gardens with plants, rocks, water, and decorative buildings with distinctive upturned roof corners. During the Song dynasty, garden design came to be regarded as a refined activity for the well educated.

New Economy

Although there were several large cities during the Song era, Kaifeng was also the center of government. For this

Officials came to
Kaifeng, the center
of government,
from other
countries and
from the far reaches
of China. These
officials enjoyed
elaborate dishes
that were prepared
for only the
upper classes.

reason, officials came to the city from foreign lands or from far reaches
of China, and this created a new economic opportunity based on a common need: food.

Like many other aspects of Song-era life, food was divided into cate-
gories. Dishes were classified according to the region in which they were
developed as well as the social class for whom the meal was intended.
According to a Chinese saying, "the emperor eats ox; the officials eat
pig; scholars eat fish; and the common people eat vegetables."[2]

By the time of the Song dynasty, the system of food classification
included palace, official, common, mountain, temples, ethnic minority,
and foreign dishes. Many dishes at the higher levels were incredibly
elaborate. The emperor Lu Mengzheng, for example, had chicken-tongue

soup every day, and written descriptions of his reign describe a mountain of chicken feathers in the palace courtyard. Cai Jing, an official, had one thousand quail killed every day to feed himself and his extended family at his large estate.

Many in the upper-class Chinese considered good food and drink a sign of advanced culture. They admired dishes that allowed all ingredients to be tasted, that were beautifully presented on fine dinnerware, and that were healthful. For them good food was a work of art.

As much as they respected food, however, no one in the higher classes prepared it. All of their dishes were created by working people, and as Kaifeng began to attract foreigners, scholars, and officials from all corners of China, working people opened the first restaurants in history.

Royalty, of course, dined at the palace, but for every other class, there were dining places to meet their specific tastes. At restaurants set aside for nobility and scholars, waiters served sauce-stewed

The Grand Canal

Rivers, lakes, and oceans were the highways of the ancient world. In China, which has a wealth of natural waterways, canals were dug in order to connect them. Of these, the Grand Canal was the main artery.

By the time the Song dynasty arose in 960, the Grand Canal was already more than one thousand years old. The first section of the canal was dug in northern China, near the modern capital of Beijing, about 400 B.C.

The final sections of the canal were built during the Sui dynasty in the seventh century. Over a period of five years, from A.D. 605 to A.D. 610 more than 6 million peasants were forced to work on the massive construction projects. Working conditions were dangerous due to collapsing walls, flooding, and disease. According to records of the time, almost 3 million of the laborers died in the final five-year period, a loss that contributed to the downfall of the dynasty.

The Grand Canal is the world's oldest and longest man-made waterway. Although its usefulness for transport has been surpassed by modern highways, rail lines, and shipping, the canal is still crowded with smaller transport boats. In many southern sections, it is as important an artery for shipping and travel as it was during the Song dynasty.

chicken or fried bean curd and duck brains to diners who ate in private rooms. At smaller, less decorative restaurants, farmers and working-class people ate inexpensive meals of fried eggplant or soybean curd accompanied by a bowl of meat-bone or fish soup. At stalls, visitors could purchase a quick snack of steamed buns, cabbage-stuffed dumplings, or fried noodles.

New Markets Create New Economy

The development of restaurants gave farmers new markets for rice and other cash crops. With such a diverse economy, the traditional system

Fine porcelain dinnerware and utensils, like the teapot pictured, are one of the Song dynasty's most recognized creations.

of barter—trading items and services—became too limited for the people of Kaifeng. It was not practical to exchange coins from different regions either, since there was no agreed value, and coins were heavy. For this reason, the people of Kaifeng used a payment called "handover," paper money whose worth was guaranteed by the emperor. This was the first recorded use of paper money.

The restaurant business also created a demand for plates, teapots, and other dinnerware. As a result, utensils made from a delicate white clay called porcelain became one of the most well-known symbols of the Song dynasty. In later centuries, what became known as porcelain "china" was produced for the emperor's palace, the homes of officials and nobles, as well as for the capital's restaurants. Kaifeng's ceramic industry became the first mass production industry. Factories there produced as many as twenty thousand teapots, plates, cups, and other such utensils a day.

The Dynasty of Great Cities

Despite the fact that military losses forced the government to relocate its capital from Kaifeng to Hangzhou, the Song era was overall a time of great achievement. Even as the Southern Song was about to be conquered in the 1270s, Hangzhou was an astonishing sight to foreign travelers.

A few years before the fall of the Song dynasty, Italian explorer Marco Polo arrived in the city after a long journey from his home city of Venice, then considered one of the greatest cities in the western world. After observing the markets, architecture, and other sights of the Southern Song capital, he wrote that "there is no other city like it in the world . . . one [that] can offer . . . such delights that one would think one-self in Paradise."[3]

CHAPTER FOUR

Technology and Industry

While some elements of Song culture and Confucian philosophy might seem harsh, the quality of life in general was superior to that of any other society of the time. This was due in large measure to accomplishments in technology and industry that are very familiar even in the twenty-first century.

The Rainbow Arch Bridge

By the middle of the Song dynasty, the population of China had grown to more than 100 million people. With the freedoms that people of the Song enjoyed, roads were often crowded with people from all levels of society transporting goods to cities for sale. Because China was crisscrossed by thousands of miles of canals, the need arose for people, animals, and carts to cross waterways in their travels. Thus bridge building became one of the main public works projects in the Song era. The problem that bridge designers faced was how to build structures that could support heavy traffic but that also allowed vessels to travel freely beneath them along waterways.

Neither of the bridges in use at the time were adequate for those demands. Level bridges would not allow boats to pass underneath; higher bridges with column supports sunk in the canal bottoms were often weakened by fast-flowing water.

The rainbow bridge was one of the great technical innovations of the Song dynasty. These arched bridges supported heavy traffic and still allowed boats to travel freely.

To solve the problem, a prison guard designed a bridge that became one of the most recognizable images of ancient China, the rainbow bridge. The first rainbow bridge was built in mountainous Shandong Province in northeastern China. Before the rainbow bridge, other bridges were washed away in spring floods when the central support gave way. The new design resulted in a bridge that was built up and out from the banks and that was self-supporting because the force on each side pushed the bridge together at the center of the arch. A rainbow was high enough to allow boats to pass underneath and did not depend on columns for support. By the time of the Song dynasty, thousands of the bridges had been built across China. The waterways leading to and from Kaifeng alone were crossed by more than sixty such bridges.

Economic Innovations

Much of the technological progress made during the Song dynasty was directly related to its economy. To transport goods to distant regions of China, waterways had to be improved. Although the Grand Canal and many other shorter canals connected much of China, vessels often had to stop short of their destination because the elevation of the land changed. To solve this problem, Chinese engineers developed the canal lock, which was a large enclosure that opened at two ends and raised and lowered boats to accommodate changes in elevation.

Trade with foreign countries, another important part of the healthy Song economy, required travel across open seas. This led to the development of several innovations to allow trading vessels to sail great distances. The first invention was the compass, which allowed sailors to determine direction. In addition, the Chinese invented moveable sails that could be positioned to catch the wind no matter which

direction it blew. As a result of these developments, Chinese traders traveled to Korea, Japan, India, and as far as the east coast of Africa.

Industry

Although ceramics was the first major industry of the Song era, the largest was iron and steel. During the Song era, iron and steel was used to improve the quality of agricultural tools. It was also used in new developments such as chains for bridge support and bits for drilling wells.

Song engineers invented canal locks to enable boats to travel through China's thousands of miles of canals despite changes in land elevation.

Su Song's Clock

While engineers contributed to technical innovations directly related to helping the Song economy, mathematicians made progress in other areas. In 1088, Su Song, a mathematician famous for his calculation of calendars, developed an advanced astronomical clock that was the most advanced such tool of its time. The actual clock was built into a three-story structure that was one of the most famous buildings in Kaifeng.

Working under Su, a team of mathematicians and artisans built an upper level that contained a sphere called "the great circles of the heavens." From this level, astrologers were able to make accurate astronomical observations from reading the positions off the sphere. On the middle level, a globe displayed the movements of sun, moon, and planets. The bottom level had wooden mannequins that struck the time of day on a clock that was as accurate as a sundial. The moving pieces of the sphere, globe, and clock were connected to a wheel and worked as a single mechanism, turned by flowing water.

One of the most extensive industries, one that had made China famous for centuries, was the manufacture of silk. The cloth was so popular that the long road connecting China with the Western world as far as the Mediterranean Sea was called the Silk Road.

Silk threads came from the cocoons of a specific breed of moth. As silkworms, the insects fed off of mulberry leaves before weaving their cocoons. Care of the mulberry groves and silkworm habitats employed many workers. In Song times, the care and feeding of silkworms was so important that the government distributed illustrated books of up-to-date information on the process. To make cloth from silk, women worked from sunrise to sunset in front of foot-powered looms and wove the threads into a fabric so fine and valuable that it was often used as money.

Although lower-class women made silk, none of them could afford to wear such fine fabric. The poorest peasants wore coarse garments made of hemp or kudzu vine. In the later Song era, cotton became the main fiber used for clothes because it was lighter, warmer, and softer

Along with ceramics, iron, and steel, silk was a major industry during the Song era. Women worked many hours to weave the valuable fabric that was in such demand.

than other fibers. Women in the lower classes spun and wove all the cotton for their families. In wealthier households, women did spin and weave, but they often spent long hours making needlework lace or embroidery for clothing.

Gunpowder

While silk was among the best-known products of the Song economy, the era's technological developments also extended to an area of life that was generally overlooked: the military. Although gunpowder had been invented in the ninth century for fireworks, Song-era scientists were the first to put gunpowder to military use. According to historical records, Song forces were the first to use a cannon. The Song military also used gunpowder to make bamboo fire lances, which were the forerunners of modern flamethrowers as well as land mines and even a multistage rocket.

Later Song scholars and officials had little respect for the military because they considered it to be labor of the hands rather than a discipline of the mind. Nevertheless, gunpowder-filled weapons held off foreign invasion for decades. Had it not been for this use of technology, warfare might have interrupted the long period of peace that allowed many other accomplishments of the Song to occur.

Notes

Chapter 1: A New Kind of Government

1. Quoted in Kenneth Latourette, *The Chinese: Their History and Culture*. New York: MacMillan, 1970, p. 191.

Chapter 3: The Largest City in the World

2. Amiens 2000, "China: Hangzou." http://w2.amiens.com/pratique/eng/china.htm.
3. Amiens 2000, "China: Hangzou." http://w2.amiens.com/pratique/eng/china.htm.

Glossary

barter: To trade by exchanging one item for another.

calligraphy: Artistic handwriting or lettering.

ceramics: Products made from clay.

culture: Beliefs, social structure, and traits of a racial, religious, or social group.

dynasty: Succession of rulers of the same family.

economy: Financial structure of a nation.

elite: Individuals or groups with great power or influence.

famine: Long period of widespread hunger and starvation.

literate: Able to read and write.

scholar: Educated person.

society: Nation or other group with common traditions and values.

sundial: Timepiece that shows the time of day by shadows.

tradition: Customary pattern of thought, action, or behavior.

For More Information

Books

Amy Allison, *Life in Ancient China*. San Diego: Lucent, 2000.

Eleanor Hall, *Ancient Chinese Dynasties*. San Diego: Lucent, 2000.

Suzanne Williams, *Made in China: Ideas and Inventions from Ancient China*. San Francisco: Pacific View, 1997.

Websites

China and East Asia Chronology (http://campus.northpark.edu/history/ WebChron). A good site with a time line and links for ancient Chinese history.

Confucianism and the Chinese Scholastic System (www.csupomona.edu/ ~plin/ls201/confucian3.html). A site that offers a thorough background on the tenets of Confucianism and the imperial examinations.

A Visual Sourcebook of Chinese Civilization (http://depts.washington.edu) A good overview of Chinese history with many links to art of various periods.

Index

Picture Credits

About the Author

Scott Ingram has written for young people for more than twenty-five years. He lives in Portland, Connecticut.